THE
COVENANT

THE COVENANT

IRVING LAYTON

McCLELLAND AND STEWART

Copyright © 1977 by Irving Layton

All Rights Reserved
ISBN: 0-7710-4832-7

McClelland and Stewart Limited
The Canadian Publishers
25 Hollinger Road, Toronto

Printed and bound in Canada

CANADIAN CATALOGUING IN PUBLICATION DATA

Layton, Irving, 1912—
    The covenant

Poems.
ISBN 0-7710-4832-7 pa.

I. Title.

PS8523.A98C68   C811'.5'4   C77-001333-3
PR9199.3.L39C68

To the memory of my father
Moses Avrum Leizer

ALSO BY IRVING LAYTON

Here and Now/1945
Now Is The Place/1948
The Black Huntsmen/1951
Cerberus (with Louis Dudek, Raymond Souster)/1952
Love The Conqueror Worm/1953
In The Midst Of My Fever/1954
The Long Pea-Shooter/1954
The Blue Propeller/1955
The Cold Green Element/1955
The Bull Calf and Other Poems/1956
Music On A Kazoo/1956
The Improved Binoculars/1956
A Laughter In The Mind/1958
A Red Carpet For The Sun/1959
The Swinging Flesh (Poems and Stories)/1961
Balls For A One-Armed Juggler/1963
The Laughing Rooster/1964
Collected Poems/1965
Periods Of The Moon/1967
The Shattered Plinths/1968
Selected Poems/1969
The Whole Bloody Bird/1969
Nail Polish/1971
The Collected Poems of Irving Layton/1971
Engagements: The Prose of Irving Layton/1972
Lovers and Lesser Men/1973
The Pole-Vaulter/1974
Seventy-Five Greek Poems/1974
The Unwavering Eye/1975
The Darkening Fire/1975
For My Brother Jesus/1976
The Poems of Irving Layton/1977
Taking Sides/1977
The Uncollected Poems of Irving Layton/1977

EDITOR:
Canadian Poems 1850-1952 (with Louis Dudek)/1952
Love Where The Nights Are Long/1962

CONTENTS

Now, therefore, if ye will obey my voice indeed, and keep my covenant, then ye shall be a peculiar treasure unto me above all people: for all the earth is mine.
And ye shall be unto me a kingdom of priests, and an holy nation.

Exodus XIX 5, 6

"Whoever shall be merciful towards his fellow-creature is a descendant of Abraham." Why did God create but one man on the day of creation? For the purpose of unity so that no man in later times might be able to say to another: "I am of a nobler race than thou."

Talmud

We now acknowledge that for many, many centuries blindness has covered our eyes, so that we no longer see the beauty of Thy chosen people and no longer recognize in its face the features of our first-born brother. We acknowledge that the mark of Cain is upon our brow. For centuries Abel lay low in blood and tears because we forgot Thy love. Forgive us the curse that we wrongfully pronounced upon the name of the Jews. Forgive us that we crucified Thee in the flesh for the second time. For we knew not what we did. . . .

Pope John XXIII: A penitential prayer composed
shortly before his death on June 3, 1963

FOREWORD

After the appearance of my book, *For My Brother Jesus*, many wrote to inform me in anguished tones that true Christians ought not to be indicted for the sadism, arrogance, and hypocrisy that had led to the murder of six million Jews in the heart of the most civilized continent of the world; for the triumphalism and vindictiveness that had preached hatred and scorn of Jews in sermon, pamphlet, and woodcut till they became despised pariahs in every country of Europe: that I had to distinguish true Christians from those who were only nominally so, who were no more than baptized heathens. I agree. Christians would willingly have gone to death with the victims of the Hitlerists and their eager helpers to prevent the most infamous example of man's inhumanity from being forged under their very eyes—and nostrils! To discriminate the Christians who risked their lives for their faith from the passive and indifferent who did not I have decided to call the latter "Xians" and their religion "Xianity."

This pseudo-Christianity has been in existence for a very long time – nearly two thousand years. Though it would be absurd to disclaim its many wonderful achievements, it is nonetheless true that it very early lost the subversive thrust it derived from its Judean origin and quickly accommodated itself to the exigency of state and imperial power. Instead of being a witness to the ideal world of fellowship and justice – the unsilenceable critic of the greed, hubris, and organized cruelty of the terrestrial state – it pulled up a comfortable chair and dipped its golden spoon into the bowl with all the other power-brokers. Christianity is a way of life; it is Judaism with a nose job. "Xianity" is a system of beliefs used to sanction sadomasochism and other psychoses. Anyhow, it is irrelevant in our century when the existentialists' Absurd has been concretized in the ovens and smokeless chimneys of Auschwitz and Buchenwald.

In contrast, Jews throughout their painful history have stayed on the periphery of civilizations that they have seen come and go, upholding against ridicule and persecution those religious insights without which human life is not worth having: human dignity, freedom, love, and creativity. Jews may not be the chosen people but it cannot be denied they are the people who chose to worship a God that embodied and approved those insights. It was not God who made a covenant with the Jews, but they who made a covenant with him. They are not the chosen people but the people who chose, and the chosen God is their grand metaphor for those values without which a truly human existence is not possible. The majestic figures of the Hebrew prophets, among whom I include Jesus – or rather Jeshua – each affirmed with varying emphasis the religious intuitions that have entered into the texture of Western civilization. Israel was to be a light to other nations.

After the Holocaust, two world wars, and Hiroshima it ought to be clear what humans are capable of doing to one another, what monsters and degenerates they can become when economic and psychological stresses go beyond a certain threshold. If we need any more lessons in human bestiality and viciousness, the future may well have them in store for us. I hope not, but when I note the unstoppable spread of nuclear weapons to every part of the world and the indifference of people to the plain import of the Holocaust, I must admit I am not optimistic. The frightening thing about the Holocaust, its diabolical originality, lies not in the deaths of six million innocent human beings but in the manner in which they perished – the deliberate use of technology to snuff out their lives after they had been shorn of every trace of their humanity. To play the numbers game as some have done by pointing to the equally large or larger number of deaths in our century among Hindus, Moslems, Armenians, Russians, and others is to be – must one shout it from the rooftops? – frivolously or foolishly irrelevant. They were not gassed as unwanted cats or dogs are. They were not robbed of their human essence before they were killed.

Some readers might be offended by the earthiness I impute to Jesus and his Mother, Mary. My intent, however, is not to offend but to disturb the unreflective and smug. If Christians wish to etherealize my brother Jeshua to the point where he is cockless and fartless that's their affair; but to me Jesus and his mother, Mary, were life-loving Jews who lived in Palestine at the time of the Roman occupation. I haven't the smallest doubt that they hated their oppressors with a passion which Jews have always had for those who want to enslave people.

In our time that passion is almost entirely directed at the Soviet imperialists who have enslaved their own people and now seem bent on enslaving the peoples of other countries. Dictators and tyrants have always tried to silence the Jews in their midst by imprisoning or killing them. Mandelstam and Babel are only two among the thousands of Jewish rebels and dissenters that the Soviet *goyim* have murdered. I am confident that their end is no less certain and will be no less inglorious than that of the Nazis, with whom they made an infamous pact in 1939 to rule the world. Where are the Nazis now? Where will the Bolsheviks be fifty years from now? Lying beside the former in the wide and lidless garbage pail of history.

To lighten the seriousness of this volume I have included several minor pieces that assault the familiar targets of anti-sexuality, gentility, social conformism, and bigotry, as well as several other unlovely aspects of our culture. More clearly than when I first noted them do I see their patulous roots in the pseudo-Christianity that I and an increasing number of theologians and historians hold chiefly responsible for the Holocaust. Anti-semitism is the institutionalization of anti-Judaism, which first appears in the New Testament and in the writings of the Church Fathers. By preaching contempt and hostility towards Jews for nearly two thousand years the Church prepared the way for the near-success of Hitler's genocidal attempt to wipe out European Jewry. The Holocaust was a Jewish tragedy, but it was a Christian disaster in which perished forever whatever credibility it once possessed.

The alert and sensitive poet seizes that moment of significant change when old values and institutions are crumbling into hypocrisy and cowardice and new impulses are beginning to reveal themselves. The tide sweeps out, leaving the strand dotted with pretty shells; the poet's vocation is to look beyond the lifeless carapaces a pallid aestheticism or conventional piety would wish to preserve – if only as mantelpiece decorations. Still, nothing finally endures except truth, and laughter is mankind's best purgative. It remains my best hope that the centuries-old tragicomic parody and barbarization of the religious intuitions of my brother Jesus will one day be laughed out of existence; that men and women will hold their sides with mirth as they recount the fantastic beliefs of their progenitors. Even today intelligent persons are beginning to find these beliefs as incredible as the mythologies of the Greeks and Norsemen, though not nearly so imaginative or poetic. As long as civilizations produce their failures and misfits, the grotesqueness of a belief will never be considered a crushing argument against it. Indeed, the more absurd the belief the greater the comfort or consolation to be gotten from it. So I have pinned my hopes on laughter, and I want to record my gratitude to those benign spirits that have moved me to hasten the demise of "Xianity" through poems of inspired playfulness. If noxious or foolish doctrines can never be refuted, perhaps they can be laughed to death.

Irving Layton
Toronto, Ontario
August, 1977

THE CIRCUMCISION

Vowed to a living God
are the seed of Abraham
though He has no reality
either on earth or in sky:
to life and its joyful affirmation
even in death camp and ghetto,
the Christian fires of the Inquisition

And though they palmed from Israel
baptism liturgy communion
and that son of Joseph and Mariamne
who taught the Jewish creed of love
with surpassing beauty and power
gentiles are vowed to death
are doomed helpers of death

COVENANT

Proclaim from every tower and from every steeple
He is our chosen God and we who chose, His people.

THE LUMINOUS BAGEL

Not only did a loony whore
from whom earlier
seven devils had rushed out
have a vision of Jesus,
and Simon Cephas the Fickle
misnamed the Rock
who saw him face to face
in Galilee
after the crucifixion,
and James and Paul

My friends, I speak the truth:
he appeared to me also
one day when I was standing
on the steps of an Anglican church
(I wasn't born circumcised for nothing)
and hailing me as if
we'd had the same pock-marked rabbi
on St. Elizabeth Street
said, pointing to the closed doors:
"Yisroel, what do those elegant WASPS
in there
say about me?"

I was frightened but I replied,
"That you're the Son of God, Jeshua,
and that you asked to be crucified
in remission for their sins."

"*Mishegoyim*," he muttered aloud
in surprisingly clear Yiddish
and hastily re-mounting his moped
disappeared into the traffic,
leaving me his halo
to twirl around my finger
like a luminous bagel

THE GOLDEN AGE OF SPANISH PAINTING

Pietàs and Assumptions, Virgins and Saints:
Someone has worked hard to put these lies on the wall.
I'll laugh in three colours at their display
And with my sneezings blow away false paint.
El Greco, Murillo, Velázquez, Zurbarán:
Fine Christian gentlemen were they all, I feel;
But did they *never* see an *auto-da-fé*
Or a Jew broken for his faith on a wheel?

Royal Academy of Fine Arts
London, February 10, 1976

THE ARCADE

No people in the arcade
and no soldiers and sailors swinging past
the lurid blow-up of Ilsa in black boots
holding a whip in one hand

Smoking pistol in the other;
the powdersmoke envelops Everyman's twin
with clipped moustache, bulbous eyes
and telltale necrophilous smirk

I am alone with my tepid *capuccino*;
the city is strangely quiet
except for a lone cyclist whose machine
shoots up the deserted street

The common imagination has been put to bed
to dream a fresher dream of life-hatred
for tomorrow's enthralled minions; no one
dreams the outmoded swastika any longer

Even the hammer and sickle is a fading dream
of sleepers who clench their fists at night
and grind their teeth: pale are those emblems
like an animal that has lost blood and vigour

But is that Musso or Minos I see ordering an espresso?
I quietly sip my coffee and wonder through the night
what new-old malignant symbol is being forged
for the billboards of the day after tomorrow

Cagliari
August 1, 1976

CATACOMBE DEI CAPUCCINI

For William Goodwin

They supplicate, they pray, their death-like silence
harangues; but chiefly they mock our presence
with their own and mock with such diverse nuance
of malice horror disdain that the prayed-to God
who made and put them here to stand stuffed with straw
withering against the walls or to crouch in glass tombs
surely is abashed, and drowns out with laughter
of his own the savage laughter in these corridors

Look, my friend, at those niches; there you will find
clearly defined what the anthropoid's uniqueness
comes down to: it is to wear grinning at the end
when the years have thwacked and squeezed out all offense
just such a subtle look of meekness and contempt
on your petrified skull. O peerlessly human
is the malediction on those lipless jaws
giving final judgement on our journey here

They mock themselves, they mock their past lives
what they were and what they did: senator
priest physician lawyer and grand lady born
white-gloved and bonneted for the season's ball;
you could say featured here for all to see
is the Christian's venom against the valour
and pride of life and that some rancorous monk
lined up this masque of smirks to mime his fury

Only the children cuddle like faded dolls
left on shelf or wall after the Xmas sale;
they alone lack the look of spiteful mimicry
and present a sad mien, an animal dumbness;
to the women death, it seems, was a trespass
or indignity, perhaps an irksome shift
from a good gossip, a winning game of cards
but the tots, alas, died before they got the drift

All these sad corpses, each one decomposing
in the slow fire of time; on the straw-filled scarecrows
faded cards giving the name and date of expiry
which translates into: "Lord, we have seen the glory!"
Did life pummel them into these grimaces?
Doubtless. My mind caresses each fleering chalky skull
even as it consigns with matching derision
this grisly harlequinade to a blazing furnace

Palermo
July, 1976

REQUIEM FOR AN UNKNOWN

Apple-red cheeks. Trimmed moustache.
Grey eyes and badge
glinting with control, loaned authority.

They leaned into my car and bellowed.
"Are you in the procession?
Put your lights on!"

With a calm
only my wife arouses in me, I said:
"I'm not, Officer,
but do you think
do you really think the dead man
gives a fart
this cold December morning
whether my lights are on?"

And from half a mile down
I heard the famous corpse guffawing
into the piled-up flowers.

Downsview, Ontario
December 2, 1976

ON SEEING AN OLD MAN PRAYING
IN THE DUOMO

Old Sardinian
with beautiful thatch of white hair
sensitive eyes and hands,
seeing you cross yourself so fervently
and bending your knee in homage
to Jesus I wonder:
arrogant and blackshirted
did you also herd
his innocent kin like marked lambs
towards those horrendous dyings
by gas or suffocation?

And did you come back, Old Man,
to this hoary cathedral
after the deed
and cross yourself
and bend your knee in humility
and pray
with just as much tranquil rapture
as you do now?

Old Man with beautiful thatch of white hair
with sensitive eyes and hands
pray to my brother Jeshua
pray to him . . .
ask him to send this cultivated
and legend-plaited city
a plague of boils
and to turn my heart
into a Rosetta Stone
on which are engraved
my rancour and scorn
for millennia to come

Duomo, Cagliari, Sardinia
July 18, 1976

SICILIAN VESPERS

He spoke well Saint John who said
in the beginning was the Word;
but, alas, *cicero* stuck in the epiglottis
and off came the Frenchman's head

Knocking the church floor, the nose
bony and crushed, it did a queer roll
with sudden swerve and hop,
the unseeing eyes calm but comical

Sweet humans, they want the least excuse
no, none at all, to slice
one's costard off at the nape
and set it spinning like a ball

Mere fringe of history's tidal wave
his blood, the blood of vanquished conquerors
splashes across this white page
congeals into monuments, palaces, cathedrals

And how peaceful in the afternoon haze
are the famed piazzas of Palermo;
how delightfully the exquisite fountains
all day long spray and play

Palermo
July 14, 1976

On Easter Day in 1282 as the bells of Palermo were ringing for vespers, some Frenchmen insulted a woman in the Church of Santo Spirito; insurrection broke out and all Frenchmen who could not pronounce the word cicero *(chickpea) correctly were massacred.*

DIGBY DOLBEN

Gifted, sensitive, emotional
he was on his way
to becoming a Catholic
but drowned
              alas
the neutral water and weeds
of the wide lake
receiving him instead

Seven white bubbles
broke at the surface
relinquishing
his last pious words
                  on earth
to the indifferent air:
"O my Lord"
"O my Saviour Jesus"

Catholic convert Digby Dolben was a friend of Gerard Manley Hopkins.

PAUL SEXTUS

That fine ascetic, exemplar
of Christian alertness
and solicitude,
is distressed by embattled Israel
raiding remote guerrilla camps

Yet nearly six million Jews
went up in smoke
in full view of the Vatican
without a single peep from any pope
or cardinal

Mgr. Frascati assures me
it was the fumes climbing
their oversensitive nostrils
that tickled their throats
and made them choke

BACILLUS PRODIGIOSUS

Because red bacteria
made the consecrated Host
bleed in 1370
                    for the sake of Jesus
their Saviour
                    they spilled the real blood
of Jews
                    sizzling them on slow fires
till they were well done
                              the more zealous
hurrying to rip out wombs and unripe breasts
with hot pincers

At the Eglise de Sainte-Gudule
they still give thanks
                              each year
for those splendid
                    breathtaking
                    far-off days
                              the confiscation
of the greedy Jews' goods
and the many incredible miracles
that happened soon after

Brussels
February 8, 1976

*The Jews of Brussels were slaughtered in 1370 because it was believed that they had caused
the consecrated Host to turn red; the red bacteria* bacillus prodigiosus *in fact caused the
bread to "bleed." The Church of Sainte-Gudule was built in commemoration of this event.*

AETNA

Ugly and desolate
the frozen waves of scoria
extend everywhere around me

The dreary waste
seems a dismal tableau of chaos
a representation a crazed and fallen angel
fixed to all eternity
under the wide dismantling sky,
an *alto-relievo* in satanic rock
to image forever formlessness and disarray,
perhaps an immense horrendous hieroglyph
baked on this forlorn plain
for Babylonian stars to decipher

Or is it a telluric Dorian Gray picture
with the movement of weeks months years
becoming ever more hideous
as it chronicles in revolting scar and fold
in odious seam and cicatrice
mediocrity's unstoppable triumph
machine-propelled and massive
in the sickening metropoles
far below these bitter demeaning chutes?

Inhaling the foul sulphuric fumes
I stare down into an abyss
to see a prodigious mound
still glowing with primal incandescence
flowing past my feet;
a single fold of molten rock
it moves slow and doomed and heavy
like a stricken prehistoric reptile

towards the scarred helicline
as I watch like a baffled hunter
on some remote forsaken promontory
its cold and shudderless expiry
on the crusted scarp's repulsive brow

July 24, 1976

EUROPE 1976

the lands
east of the Elbe
dark under the Soviet star,
Cimmerian ...

civilized Europe
finished off for good
by two world wars
Auschwitz and Coca Cola

decadent, inert
enough energy remaining
only to suffer
evil

and mountains of rich food
to cushion the fall
into nothingness

BAMBINO

It was a moonless night
though the stars were out in full force,
and the piazza was deserted
when the wretchedest stray
I ever saw in my life
came to the bench where I
and my Sardan madonna
were happily announcing to each other
the unique tremors of our psyches.
In the abandonment of mutual wonder
we were about to embrace
when the dog rubbed against our knees
and we could feel
his terrible forlornness and hunger.
My girl patted his shivering back
and stroked his mangy hair.
"Poor *bambino*! This is a poor *bambino*!
– look at those paws. Oh! Oh!
The poor sad hungry poodle. Oh! Oh!"
As I said there was no moon in the sky
and the square was empty;
there were only the pickup and I
and the miserable forlorn stray
feebly wagging his matted tail
when a light broke through my mind
and I swore I'd cut off the balls
of any man or theologian
who prated to me of God's benevolence
of his loving kindness towards his creatures
and feed them to the next starving mutt
that rubbed his meagre frame against my knee
in a dumb plea for food and water.

Cagliari
July 28, 1976

31

THE PHYLACTERY BOX

Commandant
of one of the exterminating *gruppen*
operating on the Eastern Front
he gassed
nearly a quarter-million Jews

Once only
on an impulse
he spared a young Jewess
who reminded him
of someone he knew
back home in Hamburg

In 1976
one of the grey-haired
murderers
still among us
he piously touches the memory
of that impulse
like my father
the phylactery box on his forehead
and looks out at the world
with clear blue honest eyes
a friendly light
shining always in them

THE CRUCIFIXION

Every unbelieving Jew
puts another nail in our Lord's cross;
you're all guilty for his death
each one of you, now and always

So the young Anglican priest told me,
fresh out of the seminary
his features clean-cut but severe
and his frank Anglo-Saxon eyes loving and clear

I asked him: Is Yehudi Menuhin also guilty?
Jack Benny? Abzug? Chagall? Me too?
With gloomy conviction he replied, All,
Christ's death is on every Jew

At least I'm in good company, I said
with Spinoza Freud D'Israeli Gertrude Stein
and the immortal Albert Einstein:
a great band of murderers if you count living and dead

Where could be found one more illustrious
or is the death of Socrates on all Greeks
and that of poor Joan on all Englishmen?
Ah, no, said the Anglican priest loving and meek

That's another matter. Certainly. But of course. Quite.
He was firm and though aroused still polite;
and it came to me in a flash: civilizations
like topsoil worms nurture sadists

Degenerate scum, refuse,
the enslaved cripples on whom culture rests;
the maimed and ill need one weaker than themselves to scourge
– Not Jeshua but each racked Jew is on that Cross!

MAGDALENA

Not you, brother; a crackbrained whore
from whom seven devils rushed out
founded the Christian religion:
though stone dead you appeared to her
and she cried out, "He has risen!"

Our famed ancestor, Joshua,
with a clarion blare of trumpets
put sinful Jericho to rout:
she swept the Eagles from the sky
with one wild hysterical shout

XIANITY

Brother and fellow-poet,
is this what you wanted?

The mutterings of bead-counting hysterics?
The snufflings of joyless misfits and cripples
fearful of death, more fearful of life?
The *misereres* of the doomed dregs
in every large metropolis of the world?
The hosannahs of the conformist hordes
stinking of money and respectability?

Is this what you wanted:
The grey suburban church and the greyer people
shambling into it each Sunday
you who openly consorted with whores and drunkards
and so loved laughter and joy
that you were willing to be crucified for them?

CHRISTOS-DIONYSOS

An image torments me.
I growl like a beast in a cage.
I see his phallus
Ringed by a crown of thorns
And neither beast nor god, I rage:
"Rejoice, rejoice, death is no more
For dew is the god's semen
And sheaves are his golden hair."

SCYLLA

No sailor
        I was ruined
by no mythic rock
the seasnakes long ago
having been pulled in
                changed to dry scrub
by no amphisbaena
            or hag of the sea
rising from the waves to grab my oars
and afterwards devour me

A foreigner to these parts
            I came
expecting I-know-not-what
but most assuredly
not these happy ignorant Italians
collecting and chattering at my ear
in the commonplace *pensione*
              putting away
mountains of spaghetti *à pomodora*
as if a nation-wide hunger strike
to begin next week
had been ordered by the advancing communists
to topple the government
            or flatten
the bellies of their top brass

But my ruin
        was the sight
of fat unheroic men
          squeezing out
of their skinny absurd Fiats
the ordinariness of the sunshine
           the beaches
strewn with oiled inert bodies
and the sea
        emptied for all time
of fable and grandeur

THERE WAS A SOUND OF REVELRY, ONCE

For Naim Kattan

When in Brussels
the foreigner thinks of Waterloo and food,
of the inhumanity of peoples
divided by language and history

Perversely, of Bombay:
that other fixed point
in the human compass of achievement

Of Verlaine trying to murder
Rimbaud
. . . two poets lost in this city,
its stolidity driving them to madness

Or of past greatness,
the memory of it furrowing
the heavy dark cobblestones

But mostly
a foreigner thinks of food

It must be the cosy compact way
the city is laid out
as if restaurants, houses, stores
had all been taken out
neatly baked to a turn
from the one capacious oven

Walking the streets of Brussels
their unemphatic self-approbation
enveloping me like the inescapable weather,
I feel myself a part
of their post-digestive rumination

Even the famous churches
have the appearance of waiting calmly

for a delicious brown sauce
to be poured over them

February 3, 1976

ELYSIUM
For Carmine Crudo

Carmine,
let the lame and halt
have their fantastic previews
of the world to come

And the botched
have their espials of heaven
where the humpbacked
are straightened out
and archangels with untutored love
stroke the leper's sores away

I'll take your spiced swordfish

Here on this Earth

After such delights
blended in garlic and oil
and primed with so much skill
what, pray, has Paradise to offer me?

I swear it!
Not all the damned hosts of heaven
will yank me away
from your savoury collations

Paola
July 1, 1976

NOUVELLE VAGUE

Manuel ploughs the married ladies
by the dozens – so he tells me;
in the torrid months of July and August
their number swells to the hundreds

They seek him out on the beach
lying under his umbrella
or follow him to the pizzeria
where he works evenings till eleven

And there they go bananas
over his well-shaped pizzas
charcoal eyes blazing like the ovens
his gap-toothed smiles boyish and insincere

These Emmas and Annas who spread their legs
for him have turned *litter'chur*
into a quaint crock of lies for the nice boys
in the learneries to get excited about

Manuel? He gives his gap-toothed grin
and in their hot steaming cunts
goes on cooking up today's narratives
in honour of the amoral life force

Paola
July, 1976

39

FOR THE ROMAN WHO STOLE
THREE HUNDRED DOLLARS

A crab I wish you in each lung
Syphilitic blight on your tongue;
May inflamed buboes lodge in your groin
Large as a *cento lira* coin
Forever irremovable
Though your groans shake the pits of hell;
Your wife with many ills and aches
Bear you three hundred hissing snakes
That before your thievish eyes shine
And wreathe into a dollar sign.
And if with this stolen money
You purchase cheese and salami
Let the first swallow that you take
Give you such cramps, such bellyache
Your mouth utters only one cry:
The chilling, "Lord, let me die!"
And though the festive glass of wine
Turns your larynx into hard lime
Disordered be your mind and speech
Thereafter to that single screech
While honest pitiful Romans
Declare you do not writhe but prance
And sweetly mimic to your face
Each convulsing anguished grimace
As with a loud approving thwack
They throw you coins for your droll act.

DIALOGUE

They want to talk about theology
I want to talk about murder

They want to talk about a crucified Jew
I want to talk about six million crucified Jews

They want to talk about heaven and its choiring angels
I want to talk about earth and its vicious bipeds

They tell me they are Jews of the New Testament
hungering for universal peace, freedom, agapé
I tell them they are secretly in love with death

They tell me, holding up their hymnbooks, they are saved
I tell them they are damned

They tell me they are Christians
I tell them they are Xians, baptized heathens, *goyim*

End of dialogue

AN EPIGRAM FOR MARTIAL

When it came to Jews, a pagan fool
You sneered at Sabbath and circumcised tool;
So did Juvenal and mild Horace,
Railing that they worshiped a golden ass.
Dear fellow poets, your elegant Latin sneer
Girts our centuries with *goyish* envy and fear.

IDIOTS

My brother-in-law Strul Goldberg
has made a million
selling medallions, rosaries and crucifixes
to the pious yokels of Quebec.

"Who has a better right to it than I?"
he cries, his neck red with triumph and prosperity.
"It was a Jew who started this business
though the big profits are not made by us."

"How did we ever let it out of our hands?"
I hear him sometimes moan. "Look at the Vatican,
at its gigantic worldwide holdings in real estate,
all of it made from a simple prayer Jeshua gave them!"

And just then his eyes will take on a gloomy look
as if a Frère had cancelled an order for a ton of chaplets
and his voice scale to a thunderous harrowing shriek:
"And they say Jews are money-makers. They're idiots! Idiots!"

THE CURSE
For David

Infinite stillness
by a Canadian lake
our rented cottage   plunked down
among maples and birches
my twelve-year-old son
on his cot   in troubled sleep
digesting *Der Gelbe Stern*

Documentary pictures
   Jews in talith and phylacteries
(the prescribed regalia
for angel-wrestling)
provoking   smiles and laughter
in the *Herrenvolk* soldiers
before they're shot
   Jewish children and their mothers
entering the death camps
   mass graves   huddled bodies
   the pallor and stillness
of death

On my lap   the *Globe and Mail*
gun-loving goons
civilized scum   in Belfast and Lebanon
the torturers of Chile
Uruguay   Soviet Russia   Iran

When he wakes up
how   shall I explain
human evil to him
without injecting   the weakening virus
of guilt and anxiety
how reach his mind   with the news

we belong   to an accursed species
and that greater disasters   more monstrous evils
are being readied for us
in the next century   his century

Minden, Ontario
August 16, 1976

POET ON THE SQUARE

I am flanked by guled buildings
whose dry roots go right down
into the eleventh century

A small child is flinging crumbs
at the clumsy birds
that curtsy and bob
on the ground,
strut and peck
like mean-eyed burghers

Hatless, a secular messiah
perspiring in the cold sunshine
throws words at the thickening crowd

Excited cluster of grey-blue
excited cluster of black.
I hear time's hoarse whisper
rattling through the colonnades

Bologna
February 8, 1977

THE SABBATH

Each day in our semi-slum house
We fought a battle with cockroaches and rats.
It was a draw, i.e. they ate, so did we.
On Saturday they respected our Sabbath.

Or so it seemed to me, a dreaming boy.
It could've been my father's black beard
More magisterial on that day than weekdays.
Whatever the reason, no rat or roach stirred.

Spotless were parlour and kitchen and bedroom;
My mother's hands had left no speck or crumb.
The plates in the immaculate cupboard glistened:
Perhaps the vermin had been struck dumb.

God's promised peace was in every corner;
After *tophet* there came blessed relief.
Nothing moved on walls or floors. I went outside
And heard the militant shrieks, *"Maudit Juif!"*

MARY, MARY, QUITE CONTRARY

Mariamne
you were a virgin
like my mother was
when she bore me
and my three older brothers
Chaim, Herschel, Jeshua

With an assist
from a lively Judean cock
you also had your Jeshua
but no Yisroel:
my mother is one up on you there!

What was your chicken soup like?
Your *gefilte* fish?
When you blessed the Sabbath candles
did you see Roman centurions
in the dark shadows flickering on the walls?

The silent madonnas I see
in art galleries and churches
would never think of it, my dear
but did you blow an obscene *shofar*
and add a loud Judean curse
as my mother did
and her mother before her
each time you thought of *goyim*
the godless oppressors,
the doomed eternal enemies of your people?

LETTER TO THE SOVIET CULTURAL ATTACHE

Dear Tovarisch: We shall bury you as we buried
the Egyptians Babylonians Assyrians Persians Greeks
Romans Byzantines Ottomans Spaniards Germans

So many empires, each one casting a shadow:
We became lightheaded watching them come and go.

The British Empire is the latest my people have seen
come and go. Do you recall those lovely red splotches on
the map? How permanent they looked. They withered like
the leaves in autumn and God's breath blew them from
their places. The British Empire was once the greatest
empire the world had ever known. Now its poor vestige
shivers fitfully in the gathering dark.

Tovarisch, it is not in God's plans that the Russian
moujik should rule the world. He has other plans for
you. Believe me, my grandchildren will dance on your
grave.

Out of the Far East comes your destroyer, sent by God's
avenging angels. And what will ye do in the day of
visitation, and in the desolation which shall come
from far? To whom will ye flee for help? And where will
ye leave your glory?

DISTINCTIONS

Marx,
humane ironic Yid,
is thinking of Russia's moujiks
and making distinctions

Engels, he says,
a dissenter is one who defects
or gets his bones broken
by the thugs of the KGB

A defective never defects
but stays in his cage
writing prize-winning odes
to peace and freedom

A Leningrad court yesterday sentenced poet Yuliya Voznesenskaya to five years in exile in a remote region of the Soviet Union on the charge of spreading lies defaming the Soviet Union. Globe and Mail, *Dec. 31, 1976*

DIALOGUE WITH AN ITALIAN CHRISTIAN DEMOCRAT

I used to hate Stalin
but I no longer do.

That's interesting. Why?

Why do you suppose? Because he killed off
communists by the millions!

Phew! Is that your only reason?

No. It's his fairness, his sense of justice.
He didn't confine his good work
to his own country alone but in the spirit
of true proletarian internationalism
executed Polish Roumanian Czech
Spanish and German communists as well.
What a great man!

I must admit I never thought
of that before. That's certainly
a point in his favour.

We've all misjudged him. Just think of his zeal.
He killed communists wherever he could lay hands
on them. They say at the end he was planning
another purge that would have sent more communists
to their deaths than the *chintzas* in the thirties.

What do you think made him do it
– I mean, kill off communists?

Well, you know he was a seminarian for many years.
You'll laugh at me but I'll say it anyhow. I believe
that what he learned there about God and the demands
He makes on us for righteousness influenced him more

than he knew. Our Lord moves often in ways that
are incomprehensible to us mortals. Deep down in his
soul Stalin was a Christian.

Sounds absurd to me. Still you may be right.
What are you going down on your knees for?

To pray that God send us soon another such Christian.

LADY ON THE PIAZZA

This morning I had spaghetti
à pomodora with your wraith
after we'd greeted each other
at the Piazza di Spagna

It had your perfect mouth
your smiling melancholy eyes
and stroked my hand without cease:
smiles fell on me from the air

Who thought of thievish Romans
the violence in the streets
or in one's own soul?
Once more you worked your miracles

Only when I pressed against you
did you recede and disappear
and my aching fingers embraced
a vanishing waistline of air

Love, so long as I draw breath
this city is you, and I shall always see you
sitting on the steps of the Piazza
surrounded by flowers and ruins

Rome
February 7, 1977

MOMENTS OF ELECTION
For Jacques Montpetit

who could have foretold
that here in Brussels
I would have one of my spasms
of inexplicable rapture?

my face is a flame
on the candle of my body
my eyes are pools of pure joy

was it the excellent Moselle?
the blonde waitress with the tits
of a Macedonian goddess?
the soft brown dusk on the windowpane?
the lips of my sweet love
smiling at me from a crack
in the restaurant wall?

delicious moments of Election
can assault one anywhere,
even beside a wasted corpse
in Calcutta
baking on his pile of rags:
one should accept them
with reverence and gratitude

forgive me my martyred kin
forgive me Marlowe
forgive me poor sots of Wellington
and Napoleon
whose ghostly peglegs
I sometimes hear scraping
the cobblestones of the city
when the bells of Saint-Michel
are silent

I am so filled with ecstasy
whoever touches me now
will live forever

Brussels
February 5, 1976

INVOCATION

To eat apricots and plums
after a good feed
                    a good fuck
and to write poems
to outrage people
                    with weak appetites

O my abandoned Lord
entombed in musty Catholic churches
though you exist now only
                    in this invocation
the evening flights of birds
and in ripe dark-purple figs
continue to grant me always
                              perfect days
such as this Elysian one
you vouchsafed me today

LAURENTIA

The loveliness of incorruptible snow
lying bunched on evergreens.
Am I mad that I see soft breasts everywhere?
I want to climb up to fondle and caress.

O the sensuousness of snow-covered hillocks:
a harem of naked women
inviting me to run wild among them and disport.

On all sides the winter displays
its voluptuousness made irresistible
by discipline and icy restraint.

But best I love the stillness
that coming down from the mountains
surrounds the grey trunks of trees.

When it releases me at the road's end
Laurentia will have a lover
fit to embrace her cold sensuality.

Ste. Agathe des Monts
February 20, 1977

CONTEMPORARY POET

If poems were pistols
we might shoot political fanatics
dead in their bloody tracks

Powerless to deflect or halt
mankind's snakedance towards disaster
we're a Greek chorus
      to their crimes
our lyricism and wit
the measure of our impotency

In this rotten world
Pavese dies by his own hand
so do Yessenin and Mayakovsky
      and Berryman and Sylvia Plath
Babel and Mandelstam go mad
and eat garbage in Siberia
but the Stalins
if they're not bumped off
by another criminal fanatic
       die in bed

Occasion
     for one more fiery
immortal poem!

COME OUT COME OUT
WHEREVER YOU ARE

When the Americans landed on the moon
way back then
I thought for sure they'd find Him
hiding in one of those lunar craters
I'd seen such lovely pictures of
but no, ah no, He wasn't there
Next I thought, "Well, this time for sure
He's promenading on the golden plains
and the Viking will bring back pictures
of Him holding up a big Star of David
like an African chief advertising Pepsi Cola
or perhaps flicking off rosary beads
to hearten the good Catholic souls
robed in white around Him"
But no: there was only red dirt, red sky
and empty space

Where is He hiding then
with His celestial cheesecake smile
and in the name of God, why?

ORACABESSA, XMAS EVE 1975

Grotesque
awkward
absurd in bleached angelwings
they sing Xmas carols
while their palefaced masters
flown in from Toronto and Montreal
gobble the spiced flesh
of pig and snapper
gabble
and occasionally stop to applaud
the Lawd Jeezus
they and the bewildered black children
are both fulsomely
eternally
and joyously grateful for

SUNSET

5 PM

There are no blacks
in the luminous swimming pool

At my back
the Caribbean roars
at planted beach and palmtrees,
roars unceasingly

The late afternoon light falls away
from glasses and padded chairs
and before my bleached eyes
the swimming pool
fills up with blood

56

THE GLASS DANCER
For "Bull" (D.D. Redwood)

Dark as Jamaican rum
he carefully cracks
the pale Coca Cola bottles,
dances afterwards trancelike
around the splintered glass,
flexing the gleaming satyr muscles
to rousing drum beat
to maddening trumpet blare

Working, working all the time
his jaws and flashing eyes
he fires the cruel heap of fragments,
tapping it with his bared toes
like a lone bather testing the surf
to leap suddenly on the flaming splinters,
making our covered soles wince
with glass dust and pain

Reverently enfolding the subdued mass
he tosses the burlap sack
like Homeric laurel over his shoulder
before he begins his wild dance
across the waxed floor
kicking his feet high, high in the air
and arrogantly displaying for us
his defiant bunched loins, his uncut skin

Oracabessa
December 23, 1975

FOR THE GOLDEN BOY

Leonardo, what are you doing here?
I turn on the radio
and they're playing one of your lovely songs

Bless you, dear absent friend
bless your pain
and the gift that transmutes it into healing music

I who was desperately alone
am alone no more
your aching ballad fills the bare albergo room

Here in distant Cagliari
your voice comes unexpectedly
like the remembering of your smile to gladden me

Cagliari
August, 1976

AT THE BEACH

All morning she reads
Mishima's *The Sound of Waves*
the heat and my inattentiveness
have made her sulky
the sun dries the Nivea streaks on her skin
her footballer legs
glistening like wet hairy posts
frame the pebble-held book
as yawns, smiles, grimaces
pass over the page
in a catena
weariness has made for her

She has withdrawn from me
and the small family groups
knotted under the colourful umbrellas
in fixed configurations of vacancy
and alone now
with the ancient gentle hilltops
fingering the rain-gathering clouds
suspended over the valleys
like pendulous breasts,
the slow rumorous waves at her feet
that say nothing to her
(and yet everything)
at thirty-five
she is learning to live
with the huge indifference of the sea

Paola
July 1, 1976

AVIVA

Dear wife, it is not your beauty
though beautiful you be
nor is it your warm grace and intelligence
that sweep me to your feet
to be kept a captive there
by your smiles, your brightening glance

Granted, you are lovely beyond compare:
still, unprincipled poet that I am
it is for your name alone I adore
and follow you round on prayerful knees
though, entrancing one, you should leave me
at the wide mouth of Hades

Fiery Catullus had his Lesbia
and the gentle Tibullus, his Delia
Propertius mooned for Cynthia
while the great Ovid, sensual and wise,
swooned in faultless verse
for his incomparable Corinna

I, swiftly scaling
my heraldic ladder in an ethnic slum
I, Irving Layton, with these Latin elegists
shall be numbered in times to come
having doxologized you, lovely Aviva,
whose vernal name is loveliest of all

MORNING SOUNDS

My wife and son
are still asleep
the house is quiet
soon my son will be up
and his first joyful shout
put an end to that
but now the house is quiet
I rub my cat's ears and back
till she purrs and arches her back
the only other sound's my spoon
stirring the coffee
a leafed twig
taps on the windowpane
and when I turn my head
the world moves into it
on panes of green light

SYLVIA

Enchanting are the pale-blue eyes
like splinters of ice catching colour
from the containing wineglass and the excitement
she breathes out of her delicate candyfloss mouth,
her lips a blood-drop on whitest snow

At night she rides her moped
through streets her imagination has made for her
hammering at doors she closed just before
her arrival and astonishes herself
by having nobody answer her loud knock

Dressed in trailing chiffon she is bride
and priestess tumbling into courtyards
where only enchantment will raise the water
from rusted wells and scatter the necessary bits
to feed the brooding cats on the unmended sill

Elegant as crystal, quick-change artist
in her change of moods and clothes she patrols
like a trooper the fanciful and bizarre, imaging
for a shook-up world its unshakable paradoxes
in the coarse longjohns worn under her evening silk

For the most fateful ride across the tracks
that divide her childhood from the fabled suburbs
she will subdue with an exquisite self-mocking look
she pulls her black hat down to her fragile nose
and adjusts the fatal feather boa around her neck

LOVE-LAMENT OF A MESOMORPH

For Adrienne Clarkson

1:30. I brush the snowflakes off my collar.
I wait outside for her and shiver.
The world around me, all I can see of it
is white and cold. The street is strangely quiet.

Where is she, my beautiful Adrienne?
Ah, but she cares only for tall blue-eyed Englishmen.
I can stand here till Doomsday: freeze, sneeze, and cough.
What does she care for a poor unhappy mesomorph?

Two o'clock. In this blizzard she will not come.
Go snowflakes, bring her this poem
and may it so inflame her, so dazzle
she'll think me blond, Anglo-Saxon, and six feet tall!

Toronto
January 10, 1977

CAVEAT

For Sharon

Were I an artificer
I would fashion for you a casket
made from the orient's most seasoned wood
with ornament of choicest filagree
to keep your jewels therein

But since I am a lover
I will fashion for you a poem
simple as the child's first cry
bitter-ripe as is the last:
to keep your tears therein

BECAUSE YOU SQUEEZED BACK

Because, O yes,
you squeezed back
and my hand became
liquid fire
in the crowded ascending elevator
melting gold
here we are in Paola
eating snappers
                basil-and-garlic spiced
our converse
with the three Italians
seated at the next table
billowing like light summer clouds
over heated fields
"buono"   *"molto buono"*   *"bellissimo"*

Not Leopardi, not Montale,
not even Fellini gifted and fat
could have written
a more surprising scenario

LETTING GO

All my movements
sure and full of grace
O perfectly poised
I was Mercury
flying over
a sundrenched surface

Letting go the bar
I saw you disappear
into a leaf-fringed cove
as I sank
clumsy and slow
to the muddy floor
of the lake
praying water and whorls
to erase
my unblessed love
and your phantom face

THE QUILL

I am a castor on love's quill
a rotor on love's pin or spool
I am a whirling jack
on a greased mandrel

The band that kept me turning
in uniform motion with you
has snapped and flaps noisily
on the ground

I am still turning
with the same velocity
but the motion without control
is wobbly and uncertain

Soon, very soon,
I shall stop turning
and be deadstill

SMOKE

I've come to the tavern
to wipe away
with the back of my hand
your face your caresses
and your perfume

How many glasses
will it take
before you become
as insubstantial
as the smoke from my cigar,
a grey chaotic turbulence
billowing into oblivion?

You are as unshakable as death
you accompany me everywhere
like my own death
that is waiting for me
in a villa
or a Roman convent
where guarded by simple nuns
I shall write out
my theology of despair

When the memory of your hand
lingers on my shoulder or arm
when the recollection of your kiss
reddens my lips and cheeks
and the pupils of my eyes
distend with the curve
of your eyelashes
I begin to tremble
as if a shadow
had fallen across my grave

I am the stillness
I am the chewed cigar
I am the emptied glass
I am the scattered ash on the floor
and I am the grey smoke
that wreathes your beloved image
forever and forever
though it drifts and dissolves
in the white morning sunlight
that comes from the doorway
to falter on table and bar

GONE

Lover, where are you?
The distant sky swallowed you up
in the roaring toy box
and you disappeared into its gulps.

It was a blank sky I saw
a cold dawn-white sky, suddenly empty
and so vast and overspreading
I could write my grief on it.

Without you laughing beside me
the espresso was acid on my tongue
as its blackness rushed out like a noise
to envelop the frenzied airport.

Where are you, lover?
I look through the kitchen window, stare;
the tall backyard trees and hedges
are a green unanswering wall.

DISGUISES

Bologna. Known the world over
for the arts of table and venery;
Dear Theodora, you and I
have dined this evening without stint
on its famed cheeses, meats and wines

And all evening you have heard me praise
your eloquent hands, your fine clear eyes
the poise with which you met
the ribaldry of pedants and scholars
on the loose from their wives

Italianized New York Jewess
whose Russified maternal grandfather
died a cantor in Vichy, France:
fiery Jewish particle, O solitary waif
named for a Byzantine empress

Let's hurry to my room upstairs
where in one long furious embrace
we may together rend
the nether half of our disguise
end to naked end

HIDDEN WORLDS

My young dog barks at the snowflakes:
white mice, they parachute down from the sky
in terrifying numbers, assault his fine head
and brown coat, drive him into the shed

Where he trembles out of cold and bewilderment.
His first November, his first snowfall.
My neighbour's house is sullen. Bitter.
The unbandaged shingles are streaks of stale blood

And each unlighted window stares back at me
with the suspiciousness of an old woman
though inside my head Artemis is dancing
and a god readies himself for his resurrection

A patch of snow. Greenery. On a ragged leaf
the season curls up and dies
as a surviving fly crawling on the windowpane
opens a road for us to oblivion

You are far away. On another continent.
A spider's filament connects our hidden worlds.
I think of you reading a poem, smiling
and suddenly the grass is white with white lilac petals

LIKE ONCE I LOST

Like once I lost the car key and I cursed
for ten minutes hoping it had dropped out
after I'd locked the car and I looked all around
in front and behind and between the wheels
thinking the small oilslicks the lamplight lit
were it but they weren't my curses becoming
thicker and louder with each deception
when finally I looked up
and there you were sitting at the wheel
I could see you clearly you were smiling
waving your hand and you had nothing on
and the lamplight picked out your brown nipples
as if to make a present of them to the fat man
emerging from Yitz's delicatessen
and I noticed the big bulge in his pants
in the split second I turned my stare
from your lovely breasts but you wouldn't
open the door instead you composed them glistening
on the wheel and the car started off as if
it had gotten a shot in the armature
and away you drove down Eglinton
leaving me to start looking for the car key
all over again and I knew that this time
for sure it was all finished between us
and that the next time I saw you
you would be dressed in a tailored business suit
with no more lovely words for my erections

SNOWDRIFT
For Jo

How can my mind encompass
a world of wolves
                    flashing murderous smiles
and credit cards
and you whose lips are of such perfection
they are an amulet
                    against all evil?

Mind can but can the heart, the heart?

This freezing December day
                    you gone
I imagine I am in whitest Siberia
and the yelling slavering pack
is gaining steadily on me
as my flying sled rushes
towards the dark snow-covered woods.

My fugitive Love
only when I see their bared teeth
will I fling them an arresting image
of you and me
                    scooped from this city
so full of us whispering kissing laughing
every flume ravine and avenue
lies under a snowdrift of memories.

THE PRESENCE

When I come down in the morning
nothing is disarranged, nothing changed;
the read papers lie on the floor and sofa
just as I left them before I turned off the lights;
the empty glass has not been filled
or the slice of lemon removed from the saucer;
no one has touched the pictures on the wall
or pulled back the curtains to let the light in;
no one has opened or closed any doors.
The room is an exact duplicate in every detail
of the one I was in the night before
as if someone had fixed it in a picture
for posterity.   It is of course the same room
and is why I say it's like a perfect copy
someone has photographed: and yet it isn't!
A mysterious indefinable alteration
has somehow happened though not in the furniture
or in the appearance of things; yet the papers,
the empty glass, and the pictures on the wall
all look as if a Presence had stared at them
or had breathed near them and then had gazed
for a long, long time into the black fireplace
before turning into this chill light of morning.
O Love, what are you doing in my house?
I never brought you into my house.
Go away, ghost, go away.

THE TAMED PUMA

You are mistaken, he said
I am neither lecher nor womanizer.
If I'm crazy about women
it's for the beauty
some pitying devil threw over them,
a beauty that blinds my gaze to everything
except lips eyes breasts
and roils my blood
like a delicious venom.

When the fit is on me
I am their slave, their man Friday;
they can do with me as they will
and to their absurdest wish
I am as malleable as putty,
more pliant than straw.
For their ally is not beauty alone
but the scantness of sense or purpose
I find in the remotest curved niche
of the universe;
whoever framed its empty immensities
didn't reckon on a man's reason or conscience
or the unassuageable ache in my heart.

Women and poems are my sole chance here
to give expelled breath shape and contour
and fable it with meaning.
I place on the brow of every woman I love
a crown made from the choicest words;
I dress her like a woodland queen
in trope and metaphor.
My desperation blossoms into garlands
braceleting her wrists, my sick despair
into flowering anklets.

I plug the void with my phallus
and making love on bed or carpet
we transfigure pitchblack nothingness
into a tamed puma whose whiskers
we stroke between enrapturing kisses.

THE AWAKENING

The two fight for the rubber float
their strident voices
more insistent more bullying
with demand
than the raucous waves that smash
against their torsos

Their evil egotism sullies
the thick white milk churning
around their limbs
                       The foam drops
from their distorted mouths;
like angered schoolmasters
the grey-green billows tower above them
to clap them on their heads

Awakened from her sleep my girl
flings away the heart-shaped stone
Morpheus put into her hand
and exclaims: "It's all finished between us"
and turning over on her belly
laughs hysterically into the sand

FOR SUSAN E. ROTHNEY
COSMETICIAN

Without drops or blush
you have transformed my face
I feel I must look like a god
    a Greek god
in this rattling Quebec bus
sawing its way through the wintry dark
that fills up the immense space
between Montreal and Sherbrooke

With only a single glance
and the lightest touch of your hand
on my thigh
    you have put a deeper tint
into my eyes, a flush into my cheeks
a rich thickness in my voice
and hungering for your kiss
my lips are red strawberries
the motion of the bus keeps tossing at you

THE PERFECT CLEFT
For Susan Kulpaka

You called me a misogynist
and perhaps you are right

There *are* times when the sight
of a woman
makes my insides go queasy
with apprehension

Sitting innocently beside you
at the lavish supper table
I was carefully slicing up
your speech and deportment

Even the queer way you held
the Consul's wine goblet
in your long brown fingers

And I was about to analyze
with the same merciless detachment
your Italian nose and eyes, your mind
                        when
wonderment and delight flooding
into my soul
I was halted dead in my tracks

By the perfect cleft in your chin

A SONG FOR ANCIENTS
For Jerry and May Cohen

At twenty-one
I raged under the spoiling sun
I had no time for talk
With leafless tree and barren stalk

I saw the seasons go
On sunburnt leaf and flake of snow
And never sought to hold
A woman's love, the summer's gold

Bloom of a single day
Beauty passes, cannot stay
And love like the long rain
Must come to craze my heart again

In country puddles I've seen
The moon as on a ghostly screen
And when I flung a stone
Saw it zigzag and be gone

Yet leave behind each time it went
A black hole where it was rent
And fiery ropes of light
To haul the moon down from its height

Moon and sun, the glaring stars
I saw clearly through those bars;
Now a bronzed leaf on a tree,
Let the free winds take me

Taormina
July 8, 1976

FATHERS AND SONS

Sad sad
the son dismayed by his father's
greatness

Who wired us up like that
to spark envy and hate
at best ambivalency
                    the well-earned fame
of parent or friend
pressing down the levers?

The sons of Sophocles
                    who said their old man
was a lunatic
                    wanting the old man's money
but, more, wanting to disgrace him
hating the resplendent genius
                            in whose shadow
they huddle all the days of their lives
turning over futile schemes

Sad sad
no more ominous woe
in the world

NIGHT THOUGHTS

The broad windowpane
frames my neighbour's shut window;
I see his attractive wife's silhouette
as it detaches itself from the blind
to slide down between his hairy legs

Tonight some visionary blacks are planning
the murder of a distinguished envoy
and the defoliation of his olive branch;
an acned boy
triggers a homemade device

That'll explode the bomb to liberate
his country, blind two infants
for life; upstairs their religious nurse
is cutting her cuticle
while reading Paul's epistle to the Corinthians

And someplace in brightest Africa
the lions are being thrown
to sporting Christians who dispatch them
with gunsights and extraordinary zeal;
just slightly northwest to the slaughter

Three Arabs are gouging raw food
from a stunned camel that's still alive,
a Belgian poet is strangling his mistress
Brezhnev is belching Falardeau is farting
and Herr Schmidt is looking dignified

The wind roars whines blusters
chides the highrise apartment buildings
that look like immense illuminated gravestones.
Silhouette is back, giving me a hard-on;
shall I do some rope-skipping for a good sweat

Or use the sauna? The night is cold, bleak;
a defective streetlamp throbs like a pulse
for the muffled slow-moving traffic. I wonder:
is it the city's mechanical heartbeat
or an SOS to a fortunate star?

TORONTO, XMAS 1976

Once again, brother Jeshua,
the *goyim* are ringing you in
with fatted turkeys and ducks
with cranberries and mistletoe

Some will be so filled with your spirit
they will be hauled off to the clink to cool off;
before the season is over some
will be dead stiffs because you were born;
some, gazing at your agonized face,
will have orgasmic ecstasies
and marvel at their intensity;
some will have worse or better sex
than at any other time of the year

All the merchants of the city
rejoice at your birth and crucifixion;
every groan of yours on the cross
is good for at least a million sales:
of beads, watches, talcum, soaps, sweets,
pressed leather wallets, imported cigars;
every trickle of sweat down your face
sells expensive anti-perspirants around the world

The churches are retailing the usual lies
about you and your mother:
bishops and ministers must live too;
they have families to support,
sons and daughters to educate;
The Lord they rightly give thanks to
provides, they know, for the birds in the air
but retirement pensions are in their own care

Looking through a knothole
in one of your father's boards
before he chopped it into kindling
did you have a vision of this, Jeshua,
and did you go cold all over
and let the board drop from your trembling hands?

JUDEAN EPIGRAMS

We killed and tortured you
not because you crucified Jesus
but for having hung him
round our necks like an albatross.

Baptism or death, the armed Christians chanted
And baptized the Jews in the blood that was shed.

Because the old Jew would eat no pork or ham
They washed and boiled him in the blood of the lamb.

THE EXORCIST

Three, Jeshua, you cured from blindness;
two from leprosy.
Someone had a haemorrhage: you healed him;
another's withered arm you made whole again;
the deaf-mute, paralytic, lame and dropsical,
all these you cured by touch or voice
and wherever you went
you cast out devils and unclean spirits.

Come back to us, Jeshua;
cast out the devil of Jew-hatred
in Xian and goy,
heal them of an ancient sickness.
Cure the leprosy in the souls of priests and presbyters:
their marrow is wasting away from lies,
their self-satisfaction has made them blind.
Open their eyes.

You who raised from the dead
the daughter of Jairus
and the son of the widow from Nain,
return to us:
drive out the unclean spirits in eunuchs and celibates
and bring to pass the stupendous miracle
of Xian loving Xian
as they kneel in their separate pews
and ardently pray to your image
for your longed-for promised return.

KING OF THE JEWS

Your hand free from Roman nails
and the stink of priestly incense
    I see you, my famous brother,
curving your sensitive fingers
around the deadly grenade
shaped like a pomegranate
    before you hurl it
with shouted curse at the enemies
of your beleaguered people

And I see you brought to Mount Zion
where Herzl sleeps under a mound
    circled by green Torahs;
and their jubilant cries, their hallelujahs
shattering dome and steeple
the victorious commanders
    with one thunderous voice
acclaim you, O lion-hearted Jeshua,
warrior poet, king of the Jews

THE SINNER

Arrogantly I cursed the fig tree
the scribes and pharisees,
my eyes flashing with fierce certitude
my voice made confident by rage.

"We are God's children," I shouted
at my simple hearers
and won them over with bribes of loaves and fishes
a spate of dazzling miracles.

The dead talked, the palsied walked;
the circumcised, their ringlets shaking, roared
each time I tripped up rabbi and sage:
my smile was passed around by my disciples.

"You who are sinless, hurl the first stone!"
My own tongue had formed those words,
my own sweet self, wiser than Gamaliel's.
My frame shook with the thought of my uniqueness.

And perceiving the pride I loathed uncoil itself
I stomped on its grinning mouth; only to see the viper
flee from my heel, swift with my own triumphant cry:
There was no breakout from the imprisoning self.

Till my enemies seized me one terrible night
and bound me fast and dying to a cross.
Then godlike with bitter self-knowledge and sinless
only with my last groan did I give up my pride.

THE GALILEAN

Only for one sickening moment
the houses and the hills of Jerusalem
blur into a pain dull as nausea,
clearing into steel-sharp agonizing focus
as he feels the wet corroding salt
leak down his death-pale cheeks and beard
and his dying senses track the guiltless insect
making a noisome halo around his head

Past houses, past barren outlying hill
there's nothing for his eyes to see . . . nothing;
and nothing is in the red folds of the sky,
no Father's voice to call or comfort him
though they'd raised him high enough to hear it:
only the demented noise of the insect
and below that, the Roman soldiers
dicing loudly for his mud-bespattered garments

Though no one had forsaken him, he is lost;
mistaken and lost, and dying for an absurdity:
for a dream, a fairytale, an illusion.
Still, he's not embittered; though bound, he's free,
free at last from hope and self-deception.
An instant before he gave up his ghost
he'd have wiped the troubling mist from his eyes
but the stranger's hands were nailed fast to the cross

SON OF MAN

Sometimes when I'm in a church
    or a cathedral
and I see the green constipated face
of my brother Jeshua
I find myself wondering aloud
whether the saviour of all mankind
    ever broke wind
—if only once in his troubled life—
and if he did
    was it a loud noise
or loosed among his adoring disciples
one of those deadly SBD's (Silent But Deadlys)
whose divine authorship
not even Judas could detect
    and pin on him

NECROPHILIA

And another thing, Jeshua:
in your name
all the men are castrated

They're tamed for women
to pick off
like bees made stingless by smoke

I've seen them in cathedrals
shambling after their wives
ugly and death-enamoured
all the male pride and valour
bleached out of them,
looking like white slugs
like maggots in trousers

A fine religion
that Hellenized prick
from Tarsus
made of your sayings
O an excellent one
for muliers and fifis

The bloodied nails in your hands
fling at them
my life-loving brother
before our sweet Earth
gets covered with necrophiles
from end to end
with bats and vampires
chirking
and blotting out the sun

Cathedrale San Domenico
Palermo
July 16, 1976

THE SACRIFICE

Someone in the crowd yelled, "Do your thing,
brother"
another tossed a bottle and hit his leg
two more crashed nearby into green splinters

The razorblade glinted in the August sunshine
"Right on," the crowd screamed
as the blood spurted from the slashed wrists
to make pools on the church steps

Go! Go! Go-o-o-o- they roared
at the spattered football hero, track star
star-spangled acrobat
climbing to his most perilous leap

Interviewed for TV Father O'Hara said
he didn't believe people could be so heartless
and that he'd never seen so much blood
except once in an operating room

KING KONG

An immense gas tank
pinions the giant ape.
O they've nailed him this time!

For mockery
the depleted half-men
have fixed a silverfoil crown
upon his head

At the end,
one whom great love had betrayed
he lies heavy and dead on the ground
while the frantic hordes,
flashbulbs popping light
above the passionate faces,
take pictures
of his big exposed heart
now bleeding for all of them
into their whirring sensitive cameras

LETTER TO AN IRISH POET

My dear and faraway friend
what can I, a Jew, say?
Man is the most terrifying beast
in captivity
        his zoo
being the civilized state

Blame no devil
        for the kicks
he gets killing and torturing
or his genesis
        Entirely custom-built
is his cruelty
and lodged in his character
not his neurons

When hooded men
with guns and political convictions
arrive to cut you down
before your two sons
        your poems
will not deflect them
into mercy
        no matter how perfectly
how tenderly you shaped them

MEDITATION OF AN AGING LEBANESE POET

Their shining knives
are poised
        for each others'
throats

Why should I
dance
        between them
and deflect their aim?

FAUSTEIN

As I turn
grey-haired and obese
I do not regret
the wise books
I did not read
the famous pictures
I did not look at
the beautiful women
I did not seduce:
but the insolent faces
I did not slap
the brutal skulls
of louts
I did not deforehead

If only
Mephistopheles
one stilly night
materialized
in my library;
if only I had
my sixty-three years
to live over again

RUNCIBLE
For Linda Sobel Halbert

My cat Runcible I call her
Her Greyness because she's all grey
outside and inside as well I guess
A long thin streak of misery
with a brush-cut from tail to nose, no kidding
I never saw a cat so discontented
in all my life so displeased with everything
shrilling her meows of disapproval
from the minute I open the door
and she hulks sulks slouches greyly wanly
to the bowl filled with cat food
I tell my wife never to buy it's so expensive
and anyhow doesn't bring a single thankful purr
from Her Greyness turning up her whiskers
and meowing disdainfully but just the same
keeping her nose in the bowl and chewing away
You may ask why do I keep her
when my wife is all for drowning her
or driving that unneutered nastiness
into the streets she's so irritated
by the cat's constant fussiness
like that of a valetudinarian
nothing will put into a good humour
not even the thrilling news that a cure
has at last been found for cancer
Why *do* I hang on to her? I guess it's because
I like anything that's pure unmixed extreme
and her feline sourness is so complete
an old curmudgeon would die of envy
seeing how she exhibits it over choice ground meat
or a saucer full of fresh cream
that I place in front of her twitchy nose
to see how far she'll take her disapproval
of a world she never asked to be littered in,

her dislike of it so absolute
there's an unmistakable hint of greatness in it
Also she does remind me of my dead mother
and of certain other people whose names
are in my diaries 1943-1976
and anyway my two favourite ancients
honoured above all others, Homer himself,
have always been Archilochus and Thersites
two Greeks who bitched themselves into immortality

THE DAY GOD WAS LOOKING AFTER
THE LITTLE SPARROW

Then the quake struck
and everybody was crying and shouting
warning the neighbourhood
the tidal wave
was coming at us

I tried to gather
my five children
into my arms:
the waves swept us out
of the house
like straw

When I found my arms
were empty
I wanted to shout
and curse my misery
but I had no more voice
and I was too shocked to cry

My eyes were open
and then I saw my little girl
her small fingers waving
for help that never came

That is how I lost my little girl

Manila
August 18, 1976

HOMECOMING

Nor have I seen a toad
                 not a single one
a welcoming grass-snake
whipping past my feet   a hare
though my backside has warmed
the field-rock
            me silent and concentrated
as itself
birches, yes   maples, yes   larches, yes
lots of those
           all around me
and yellow butterflies
weaving invisible mends
between hedge and hedge
                the sky
as I remember it
blue and over-arching
not muffling the insect noises

I shall wait
          for the afternoon
to yawn
          and let fly out
a mouthful of familiar birds
for a grasshopper
             to imagine my knees
a windflower
          and welcome me back
with record-breaking hop
            a mosquito
to circle my head
          and move off
making a pleased noise

Minden, Ont.
August 19, 1976

A WALK TO NOWHERE

Early morning. More quiet than a prayer
the mortgaged cottages are still asleep. I catch
the first faint whisperings of water and bush

The cool silent road. My confident foot-tread.
The leaf-flecks I step on growing bigger
as the hour launders the blueness out of the air

A lone butterfly paddling towards the hedge;
frail dust-disturber, yellow-wing'd petal
fluttering for entry into the world of green

However far I go the wheel-tracks keep after me
unrolling as I walk and encircling the lake
like a noose waiting to be pulled tight with cottages

While peering across their fenced-in reservations
the campers discreetly arrange their caravans
against their pensioned-off ghosts in office and home

Caribou Lodge
August 23, 1976

MINDEN, ONT.

Foxy Lady
your yellow coat in the tall green grass
your joyous leaps and bounds
that carried the sunlight on your back
from stone to stone
was too much for my neighbours
in their rented cottages darkening mine

They never saw you
but tight-assed Ontarioan Prots
are a queer breed of canine:
their fine Loyalist nostrils sniffed
the pleasure we had in our walks
and they rushed off
snuffling with complaint
Damn them, eh Foxy Lady
may they piss razorblades
all this week

Tomorrow morning
I'll have to take you to kennels
and leave you there
Bark loud and long and clear, my girl
bark them to a bad year
while I return to Caribou Lodge
to fix forever in my mind
their happy protestant faces

CALLIGRAPHY

The red ants
were all over
the dusty dead halved centipede

The other half was nowhere
to be seen:
had the fifty legs walked off
to a separate existence?

Que sabe?
But the half I saw
sun-curved and slightly raised
threw the shadow of a horseshoe
on the white gravelly road
—of a small but perfect U

THE FIRE-GUTTED CHURCH ON AVENUE ROAD

Why should the good Lord want to burn down His house?
   Each Sunday they gave Him their love
And promised Him more should that not be enough;
   Bent their knees, said their prayers

And did all they are supposed to for a God.
   Even now, even through this murk
They see His fierce concern; in His handiwork
   They feel His presence and are awed

The windows are all stained by His radiant smoke
   And His bright fires blacked these stones;
Over the burnt altarcloth the wind intones
   And the deacon wears a strange look

A PSALM OF DAVID

"Pour out thy indignation upon them
and let thy burning anger overtake them,
May their camp be a desolation,
let no one dwell in their tents.
For they persecute him whom thou has smitten,
and him whom thou hast wounded, they afflict
still more."
—*Psalm 69*

The hour is desperate
what if Jahweh
came out
        of a desert whirlwind
to bestir himself
for his hard-pressed people
dumping
        the hate-filled Palestinians
into Libyan oil wells
before igniting them
with his lightning anger?

And all the other
charming affable volatile voluble
murderous Arabs
—Syrians Jordanians Egyptians Iraqis

Surely he has cached enough
oil deposits
        in Kuwait
for just such an emergency.

EL DIABLO

For Nicholas Haines

Always there's a smell of sulphur
clings to him, a subtle fume,
even when we're out-of-doors
having our drinks on the terrace
or walking arm-in-arm in the garden
and his right sleeve, I've noticed, is singed.
He has trouble keeping his pipe lit
striking one futile match after another
and I always marvel at that
for I swear there have been times
I saw small flames shoot from his mouth.
It's the chastity in his evilness
that fascinates me, a purity
only absolute egotism may achieve;
it has the rightness of a cobra bite
and therefore a kind of beauty
that mesmerizes before the mortal sting.
A Westmount patrician, in his malignity
there is shame but never guilt
as for an odious blotch, an ugliness,
never a falling away from grace;
for he assumes its necessary place
in the order of things, like the flatworms
ignorant of the Milky Way, the sun's orbitings
or the Dionysian Christ on a crotch
he offers as saviour of our corrupt world
swiftly racing downhill to disaster
if only it takes His stiffened rod
for steerer; and then I think he's mad
not evil till I look into the ashtray
and see the heap of trim white bodies
of the beautiful boys he's ruined.

HEINRICH HEINE

I dreamt that I was Satan
Being warmed by molten stones
And critics who had scorned me
Had to memorize my poems

As pious Jews read their Scroll
Book to book the year around
They recite my brilliant lines,
Not a bad one can they find

Day in day out till time ends
To reclaim their wizened souls
They sing my deathless *Lieder*
And they dance on fiery coals

THE BALD TARTAR

I'll roll the sights I see
into a hard pellet
and with it knock out your eye
you must see what I see
or not at all
you have one more chance
and one more eye

FREAKS
For Beth Marcilio

Ordinary people are weird
my wife says a look of terror comes
into my blue eyes when one of them
addresses me in the recreation room
or on the beach where I stretch out on the sand
exposed and helpless: "I burn to a crisp
if I'm out in the sun for more than an hour/
the Dodgers can't make it/what do you say fella?"
I'm not quick-witted enough to come back
with a zinging answer and begin to stammer
as if Queen Elizabeth had spoken to me
or that beautiful Jewess Elizabeth Taylor
and my tongue is a pegleg going down
on a wet unsanded surface only more so
since they're women and we all know
their hormones prevent their being normal
and perfectly ordinary so what *does*
one say to one of these inoffensive
bland nondescript unimportant hard-working
mortals in striped trunks pink and smoking
a cigar who wants to reel you into a conversation
about auto makes the weather baseball how he
came back one night to his hotel room blotto
smashed pie-eyed pissed to the gills Boy
did I tie one on! after the class reunion
only it wasn't his room he let himself into
he must've taken somebody else's key
and the woman you'd better believe this fella
it's bible truth was on the sofa naked
masturbating in front of a mirror
etcetera ... etcetera ...

O CURELESS RAPTURE

Take it from one who has observed the malady
at first hand: it's incurable
you'd have a better chance with poliomyelitis
or nowadays even with cancer

Check for these symptoms
fluent articulateness without individuality and style
cleverness that falls always short of insight or intuition
and therefore dooms you to be forever
a Johnny-come-lately in the world of culture and thought
a boring earnestness which is the national brandsign
for the ownership and control of your psyche
by the democratic *cacoëthes* lodged in your lower bowel

A superlative litmus test is anti-Americanism
check at once
or a penchant for writing lifeless poems
coupled with an unfailing inability amounting to genius
to spot originality or greatness
above everything
note any excessive adulation in yourself
for the tritely new, the fashionably old
and observe the telltale lack of passion
in everything you write say and do
there is, alas, no serum for blandness, no antibiotic

Your condition, let's face it, is hopeless
but you won't die from it either
indeed to put a good face on the matter
I can see you ending your life
in one of the country's famous learneries
not as caretaker, no! no! but as an eminent Ph.D. in Bantulit
or as a politician in Ottawa
or even perhaps – why not? –
as the renowned editor of the Oakville *Standard*

SOVIET BROILERISM 2000 AD

In gowns . . . jackets of red velveteen
in T-shirts . . . jeans
queuing up for concerts
the best-selling novels
art exhibits

All the same
. . . broilers!

After the carefully measured quanta
of feed, warmth, and light
after the weak chirps
one thick sauce
                      drips
over them all

But the young plantains
even these weeds
grow to their appointed height
under the open sky

INNOCENTS

People born deaf
have innocent lovely faces
are innocent and lovely

Never having once heard
the inflexions
of sarcasm and irony

THOUGHTS ON TITLING MY NEXT BOOK "BRAVO, LAYTON"

Now my worst enemies
and the proudest men on earth
senators kings presidents MP's
as well as famous athletes and cosmonauts
will have to fall into line
with everybody else on this planet
and shout "Bravo, Layton"
when they ask for my book

Librarians book collectors and book salesmen
from Toronto all the way to Peking
will acclaim me fervently
without giving the matter a second thought
as if the huzzas were the most expected
most ordinary thing in the world

And those who hate my guts
and anyone I owe money to or a favour
all my ex-mistresses and ex-friends
                              in fact
anyone who would like to maim or murder me
because I am famous rich sexy
generous compassionate life-loving
adored by women and children
and irrepressibly creative
will be startled out of their minds
when they're standing in a bookstore
or close to a kiosk
to hear a complete stranger
suddenly cry out, "Bravo, Layton"

Even the primmest Canucky shmuck
without reading a single line
now must begin his hostile review

by paying me homage: "Bravo, Layton" . . .
and though I'm too stupendously great
to have any
                rival poets
and hordes of Canada Council poetasters
lifted from obscurity and on their way
to oblivion
will have to exclaim with everyone else
in this country, "Bravo, Layton"

Finally the terrestrial paeans
reaching him, Saint Pinchas himself
will open the pearl-studded gates
and his "Bravo, Layton"
followed by a clamorous roar of trumpets
will rebound from heaven to heaven
till the ascendant echoes
fall on the most exalted floor of all
where snoring on his onyx throne,
his sprawled-out legs glistening with constellations,
the King of Kings is roused from a post-prandial nap
that has lasted trillions and trillions
and trillions of light-years
to mumble softly into his golden beard
"Bravo, Layton . . . Bravo, Layton . . . Bravo, Layton"

REVIEW OF "BRAVO, LAYTON"

Boo, Layton! Boo, Layton, Boo . . .
In this book Layton has stripped away
all the trappings of restraint and decency
and has revealed himself to be
the uninhibited megalomaniac
we always suspected he was.
Still, after the ponderous *For My Brother Jesus*
which revealed a streak of ugly racism
hitherto kept under strict control
it's something to be thankful for
that he has come down from his chosen Mount Sinai
to give us in his latest volume
some entertaining light verse and doggerel
which to one reviewer at any rate
appears to be where the talent
of this vastly over-rated author lies.
So taking a hint from the title
of one of E. M. Forster's books
Two Cheers for Democracy
a collection of civilized essays he
might profitably study for their urbanity,
mellow wisdom, and grace,
let me conclude this brief notice
of the thirty-third—or is it the thirty-fourth?—volume
of this rowdy silly tortured tender
feisty outrageous posturing egotistical
and somewhat pathetic excuse for a poet
(only if a repeater delivering bullets
each time with the same speed and noise
is said to be fertile may Layton's
much-advertised claim to fertility
be seriously considered)
by resisting the near-irresistible urge
to go the whole way
and to call only for "Two Boos for Layton"

hoping we've not allowed ourselves
to be trapped by his latest manifestation
of vulgar taste into following it
by an equally vulgar exhibition of our own
and that we've left in our readers' ears
the sound of only one hand clapping.

THE PROGRESS OF POESY

I shall write a marvelous poem
and trade it for a gun
I shall compose another one
and barter it for an automatic
I shall write a superb sonnet
and exchange it for a small bomb
I shall set down a modern Paradise Lost
and trade it for a bazooka
I shall indite a magnificent ode
and swap it for a howitzer
finally for a masterpiece, my best poem
I shall demand the newest cannon

When I have a large enough arsenal
to protect me from the murderous goons
springing up everywhere around me
I shall start over again
and write a simple joyous lyric
extolling my love's black eyebrows

COME CLOSER, BROTHERS

Yoo-hoo . . . yoo-hoo . . . not a sound
God has moved to another universe
and taken an unlisted number
On our poor raft of Earth
we are spinning in a whirlpool of space
alongside trillions and trillions
of humanless mudlumps
we are spinning in a terrifying silence
O infinite ocean of nothingness!
are we ill with spacesickness
that our hands reach out to throttle and kill?
Yids Wasps Krauts Russkies
Niggers Polacks slant-eyed Chinks Wops
don't wait for the Martians
or the Venusians
with ears shaped like antennae,
computers in their eagle claws:
come closer, Brothers

ACKNOWLEDGEMENTS

For permission to reprint poems in this volume grateful acknowledgement is made to the editors of the following periodicals: *Exile, Northern Journey, Chatelaine, Waves, The Jewish Chronicle, Chicago Review*, and *Ontario Review*.